Holiday Classics

VOLUME 2

Easy Multi-Level Holiday Solos

Arrangements by
Jennifer Eklund

PIANO PRONTO PUBLISHING

PianoPronto.com

Holiday Classics: Volume 2

Jennifer Eklund

Copyright ©2018 by Piano Pronto Publishing, Inc. (ASCAP)

All rights reserved. The compositions, arrangements, text, and graphics in this publication are protected by copyright law. No part of this work may be duplicated or reprinted without the prior consent of the author.

ISBN: 978-1-64266-016-6

Printed in the United States of America.

Piano Pronto Publishing, Inc.
PianoPronto.com

Holiday Classics

Volume 2

TABLE OF CONTENTS

UP ON THE HOUSETOP (Version 1) 1
UP ON THE HOUSETOP (Version 2) 3
UP ON THE HOUSETOP (Version 3) 5
I SAW THREE SHIPS (Version 1) 7
I SAW THREE SHIPS (Version 2) 9
I SAW THREE SHIPS (Version 3) 11
SING WE NOW OF CHRISTMAS (Version 1). 13
SING WE NOW OF CHRISTMAS (Version 2) 15
SING WE NOW OF CHRISTMAS (Version 3) 17
AULD LANG SYNE (Version 1). 19
AULD LANG SYNE (Version 2). 21
AULD LANG SYNE (Version 3). 23
WE THREE KINGS (Version 1) 25
WE THREE KINGS (Version 2) 27
WE THREE KINGS (Version 3) 29
WE WISH YOU A MERRY CHRISTMAS (Version 1). 31
WE WISH YOU A MERRY CHRISTMAS (Version 2) 33
WE WISH YOU A MERRY CHRISTMAS (Version 3) 35
UKRAINIAN BELL CAROL (Version 1) 37
UKRAINIAN BELL CAROL (Version 2) 39
UKRAINIAN BELL CAROL (Version 3) 41
THE FIRST NOEL (Version 1) 43
THE FIRST NOEL (Version 2) 45
THE FIRST NOEL (Version 3) 47
JOY TO THE WORLD (Version 1) 49
JOY TO THE WORLD (Version 2) 51
JOY TO THE WORLD (Version 3) 53
O HOLY NIGHT (Version 1). 55
O HOLY NIGHT (Version 2). 57
O HOLY NIGHT (Version 3). 59

Arrangements by
Jennifer Eklund

Up on the Housetop
Version 1

Benjamin Hanby
Arr. Jennifer Eklund

Joyful & light

Copyright © 2018 Piano Pronto Publishing, Inc. (ASCAP)
All Rights Reserved | PianoPronto.com

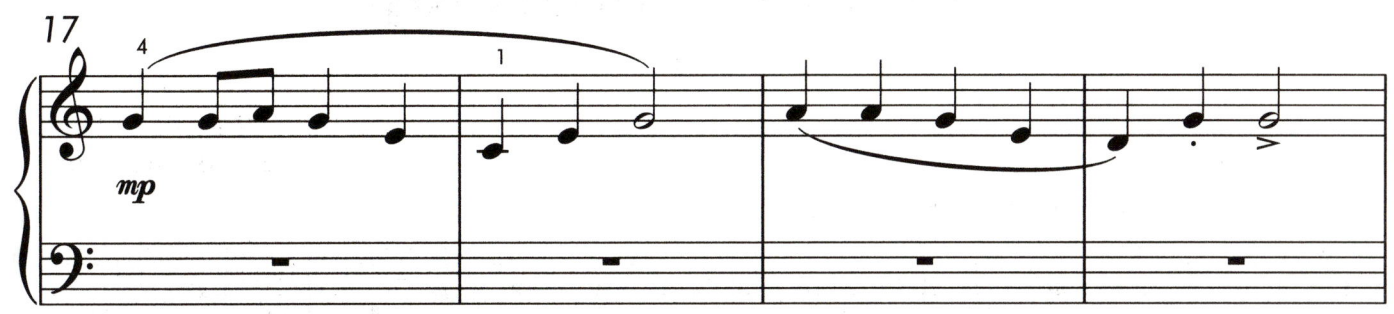

Up on the Housetop
Version 2

Benjamin Hanby
Arr. Jennifer Eklund

Joyful & light

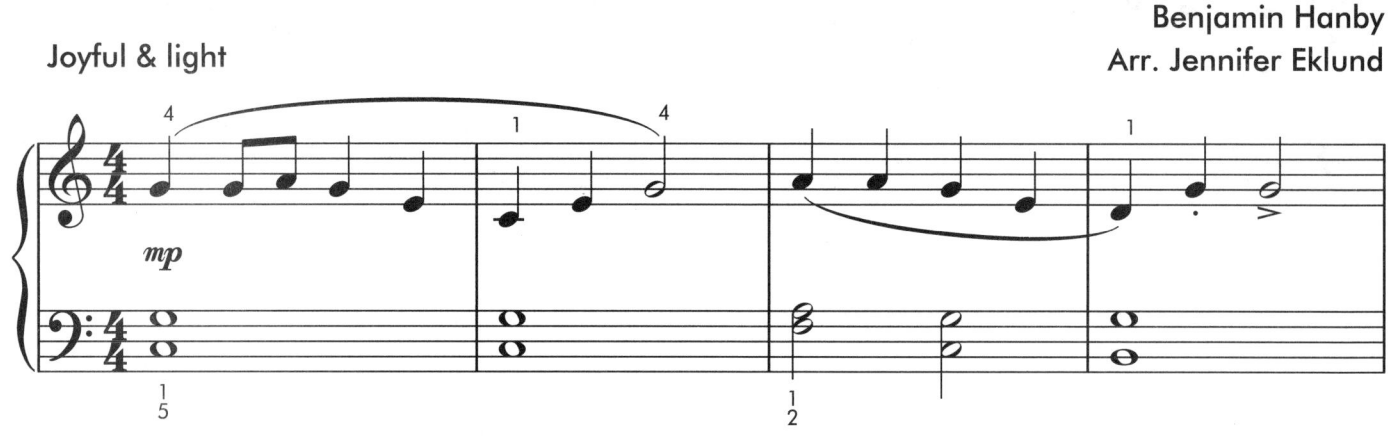

Up on the Housetop
Version 3

Benjamin Hanby
Arr. Jennifer Eklund

Joyful & light

Copyright © 2018 Piano Pronto Publishing, Inc. (ASCAP)
All Rights Reserved | PianoPronto.com

I Saw Three Ships
Version 1

Traditional
Arr. Jennifer Eklund

Lilting along

with pedal

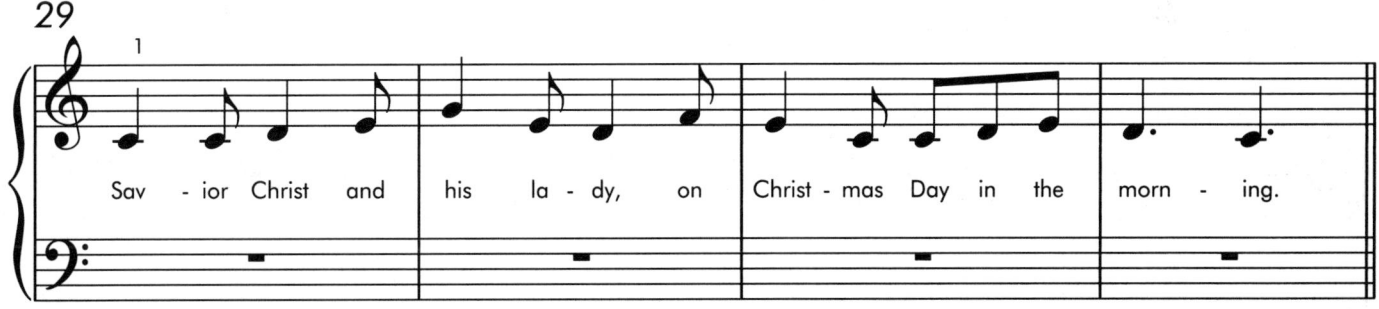

I Saw Three Ships
Version 2

Traditional
Arr. Jennifer Eklund

Lilting along

with pedal

I Saw Three Ships
Version 3

Traditional
Arr. Jennifer Eklund

Lilting along

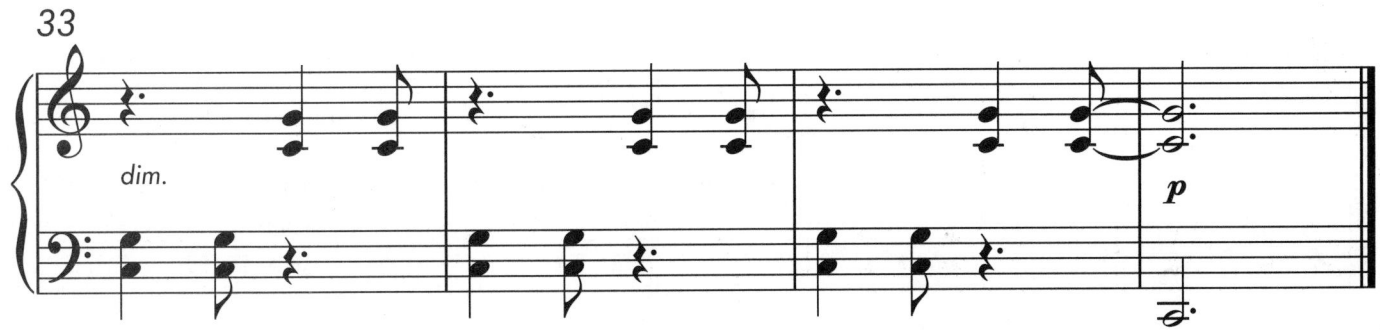

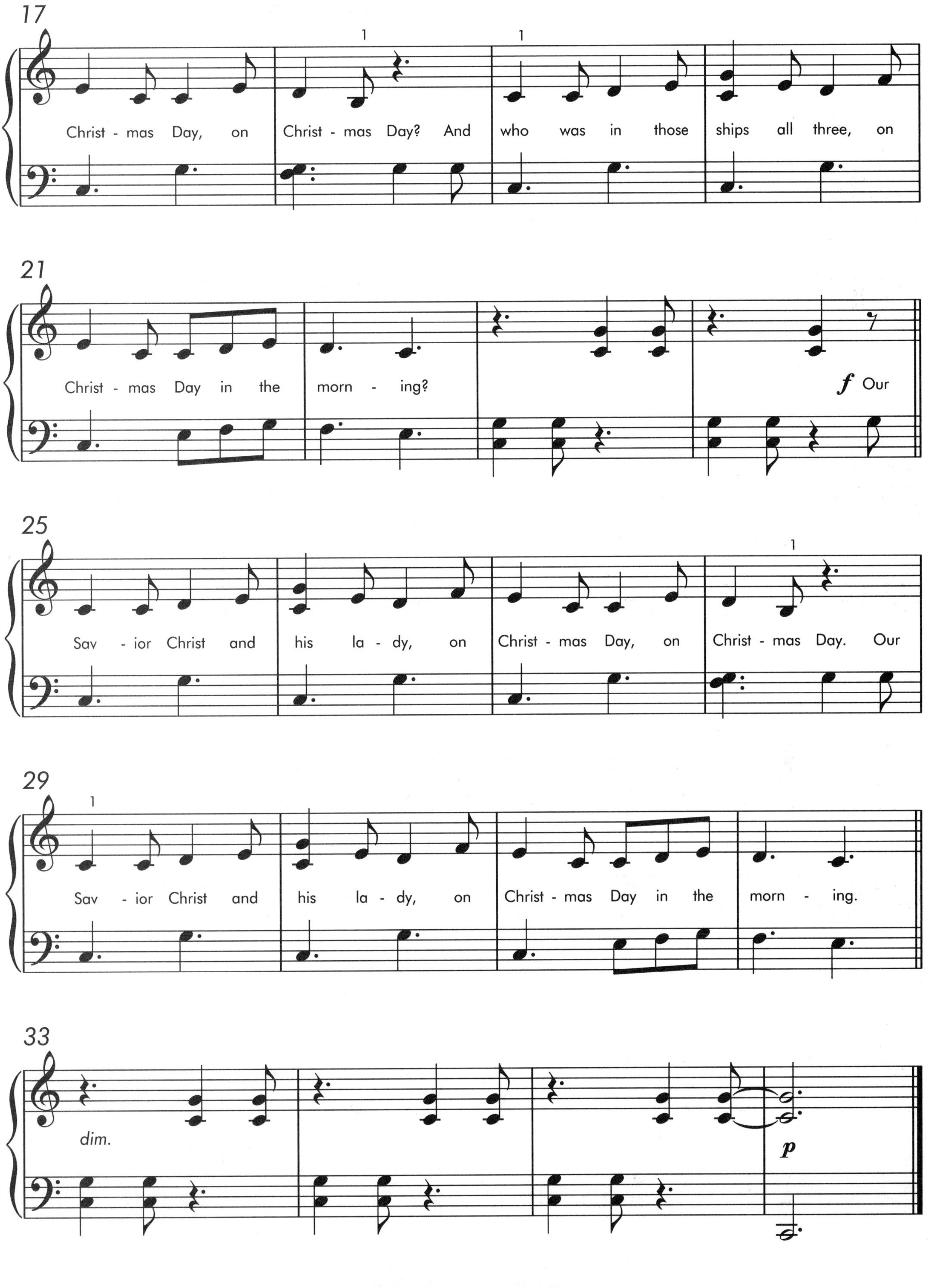
17
1
1
Christ - mas Day, on Christ - mas Day? And who was in those ships all three, on
21
Christ - mas Day in the morn - ing?
f Our
25
1
Sav - ior Christ and his la - dy, on Christ - mas Day, on Christ - mas Day. Our
29
1
Sav - ior Christ and his la - dy, on Christ - mas Day in the morn - ing.
33
dim.
p

Sing We Now of Christmas

Version 1

French Carol
Arr. Jennifer Eklund

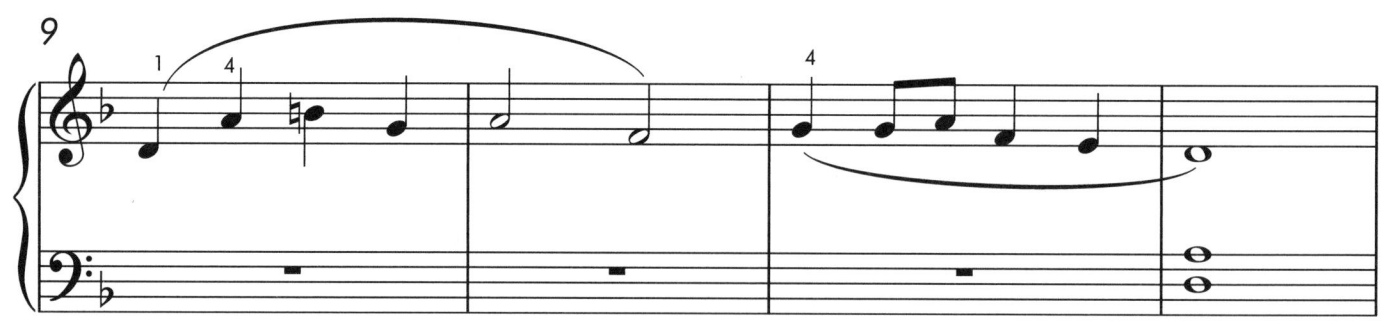
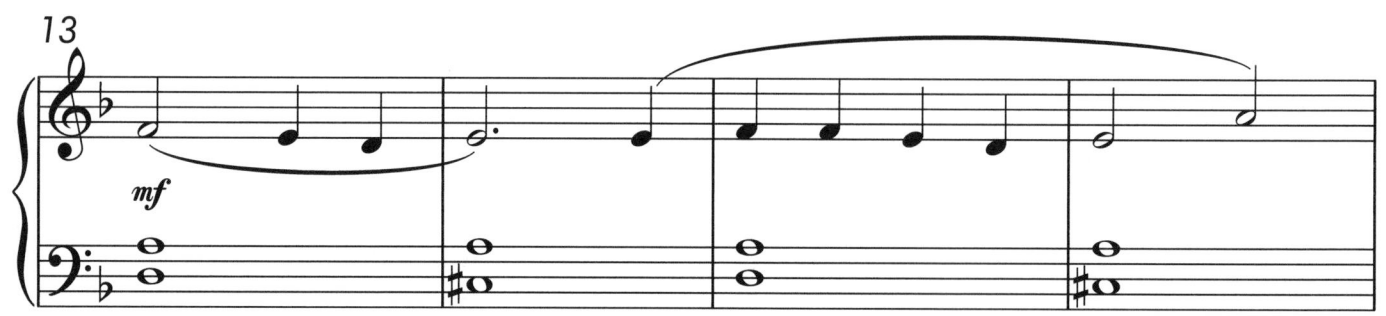

Copyright © 2018 Piano Pronto Publishing, Inc. (ASCAP)
All Rights Reserved | PianoPronto.com

Sing We Now of Christmas
Version 2

French Carol
Arr. Jennifer Eklund

Sing We Now of Christmas
Version 3

French Carol
Arr. Jennifer Eklund

Auld Lang Syne
Version 1

Traditional
Arr. Jennifer Eklund

Expressively

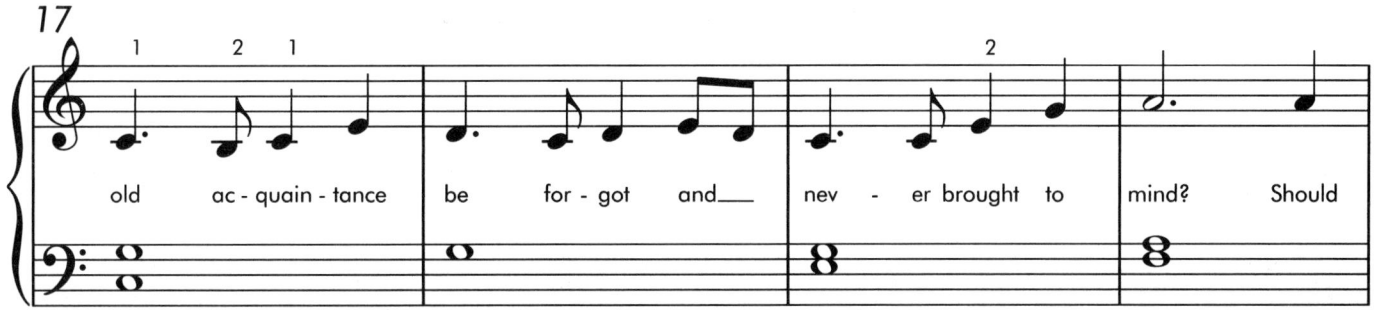
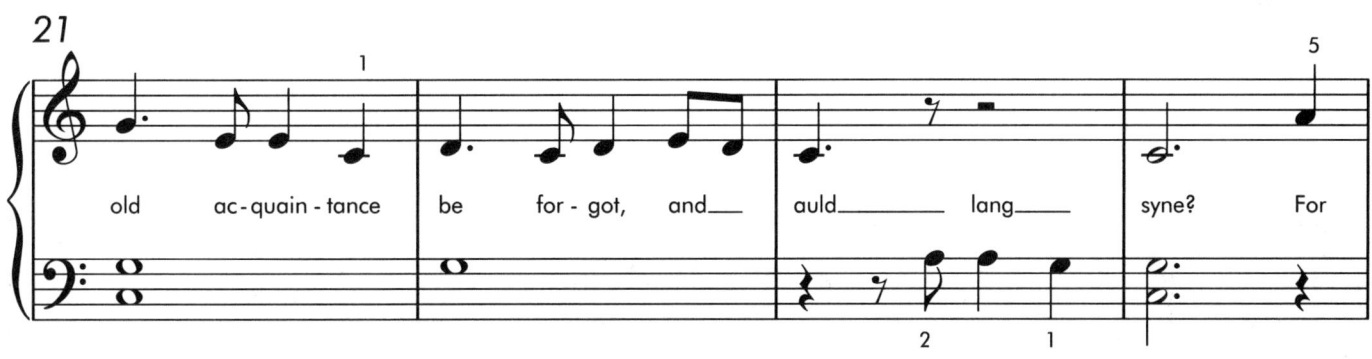

Auld Lang Syne
Version 2

Traditional
Arr. Jennifer Eklund

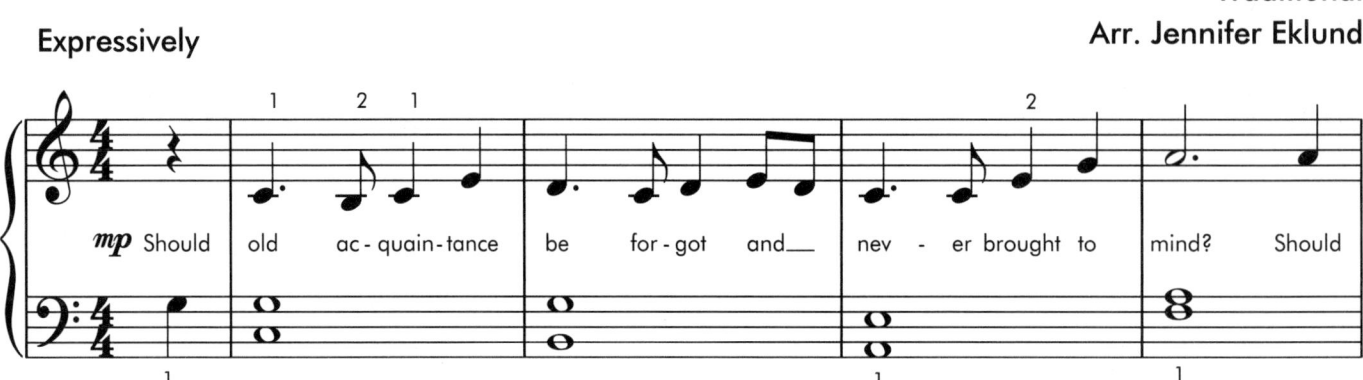

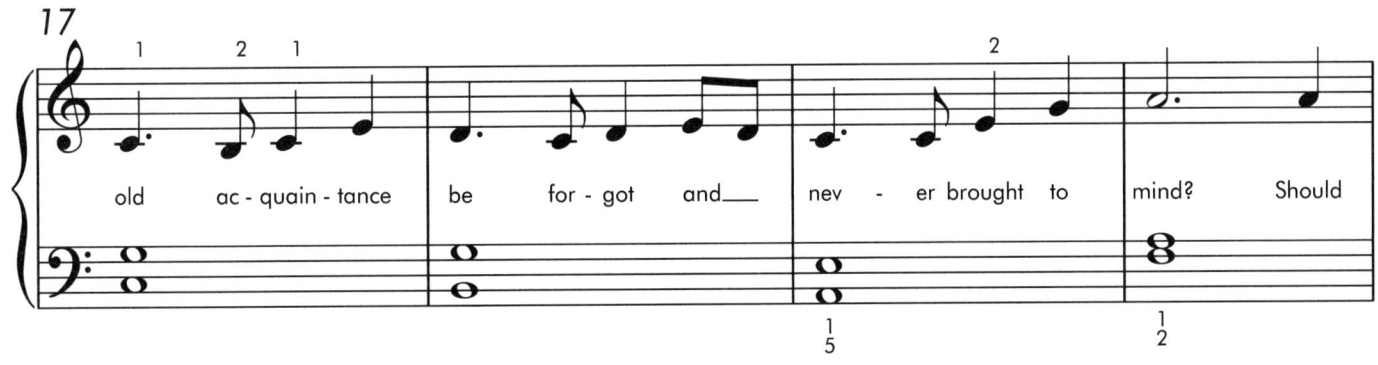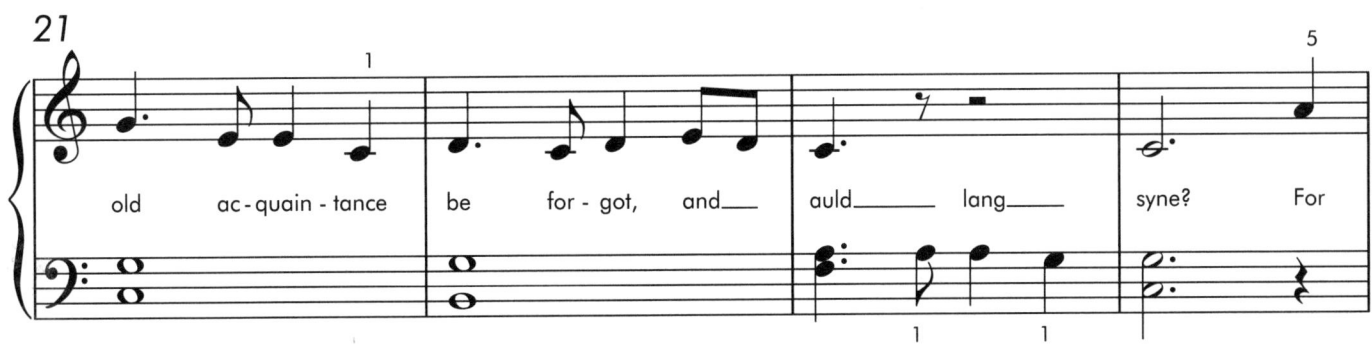

Auld Lang Syne
Version 3

Traditional
Arr. Jennifer Eklund

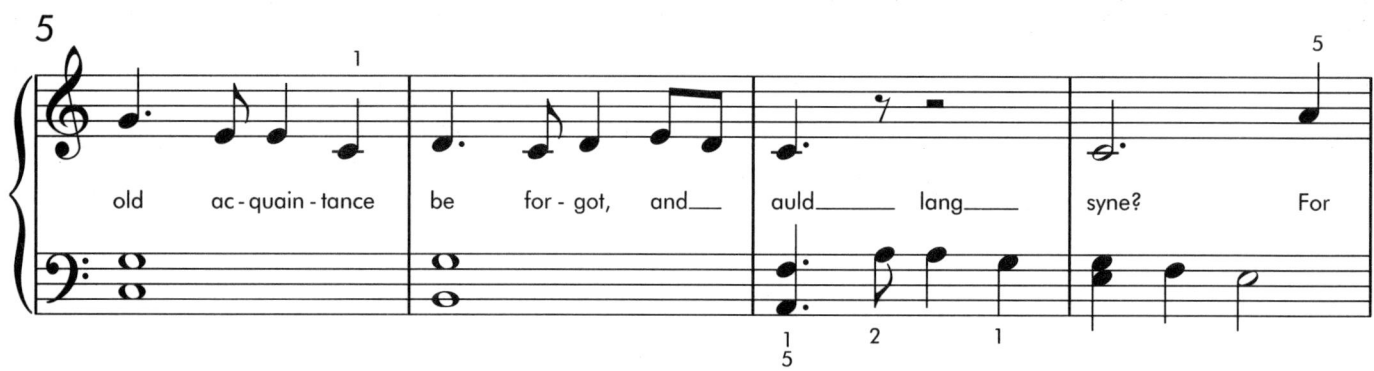

Copyright © 2018 Piano Pronto Publishing, Inc. (ASCAP)
All Rights Reserved | PianoPronto.com

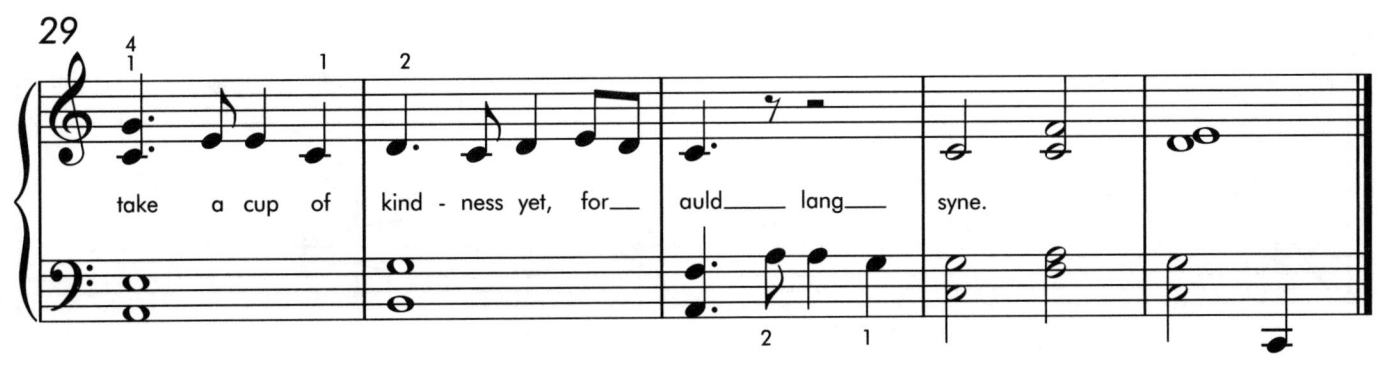

We Three Kings
Version 1

Traditional
Arr. Jennifer Eklund

Slow & smooth

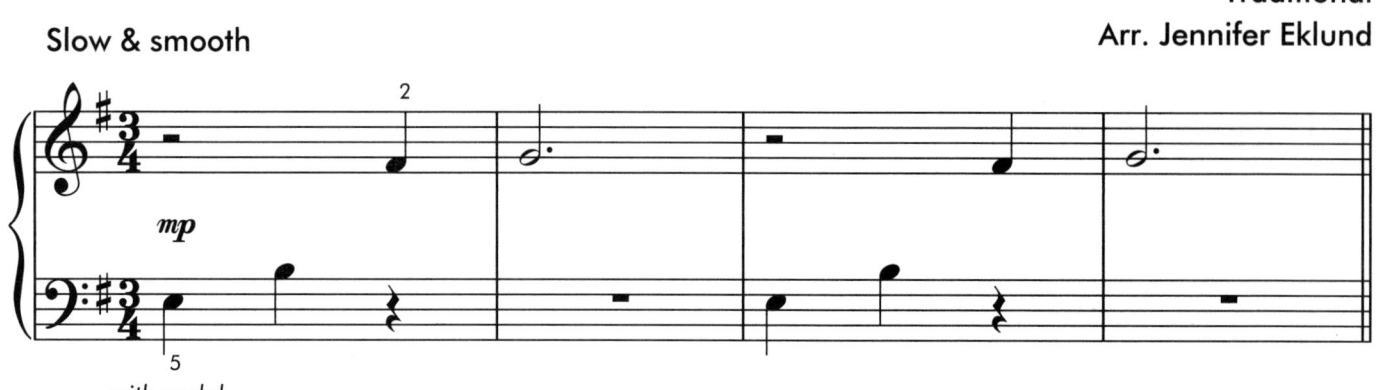

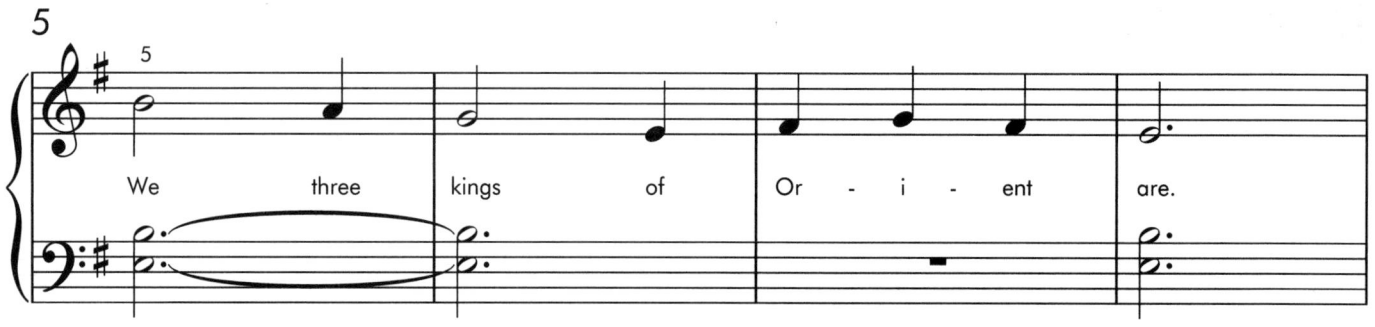

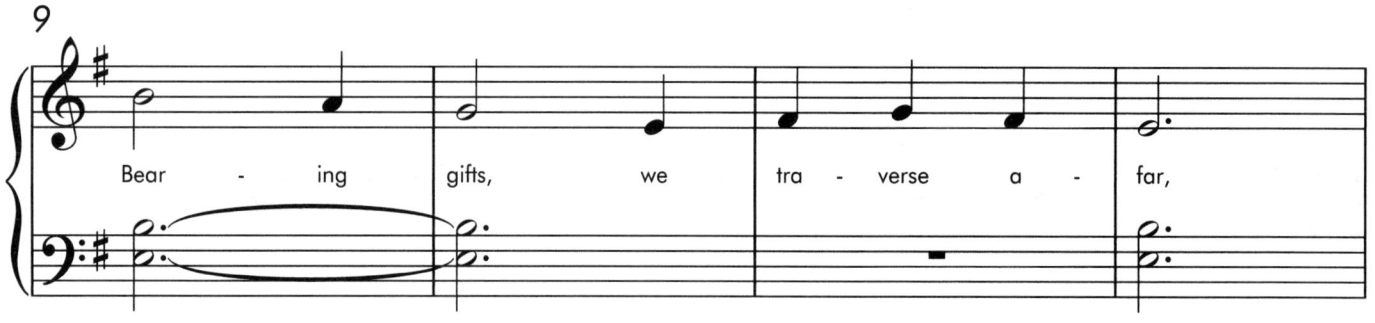

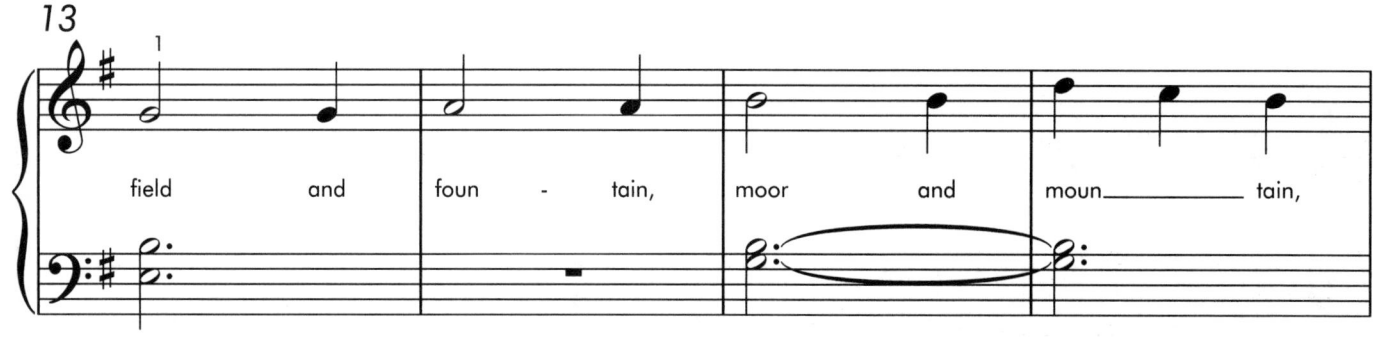

We Three Kings
Version 2

Traditional
Arr. Jennifer Eklund

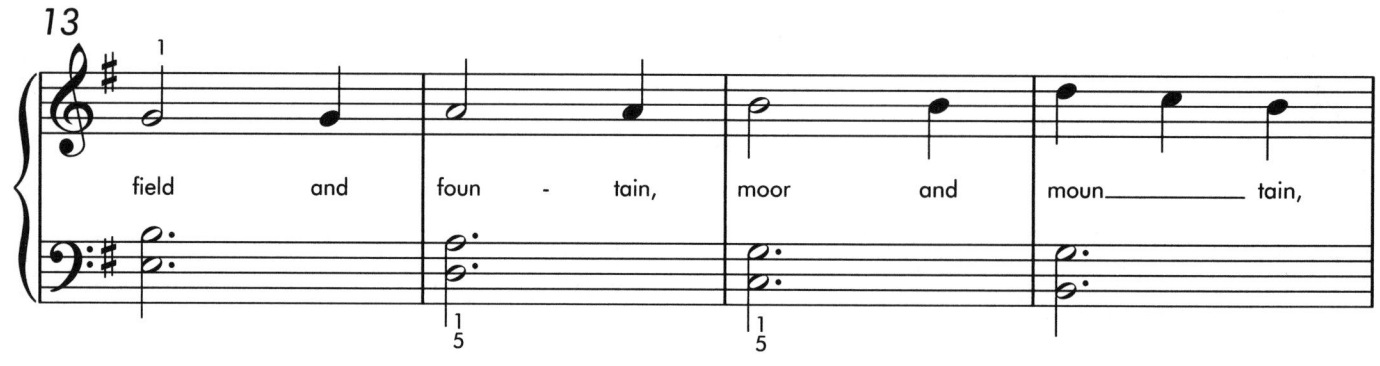

We Three Kings
Version 3

Traditional
Arr. Jennifer Eklund

Slow & smooth

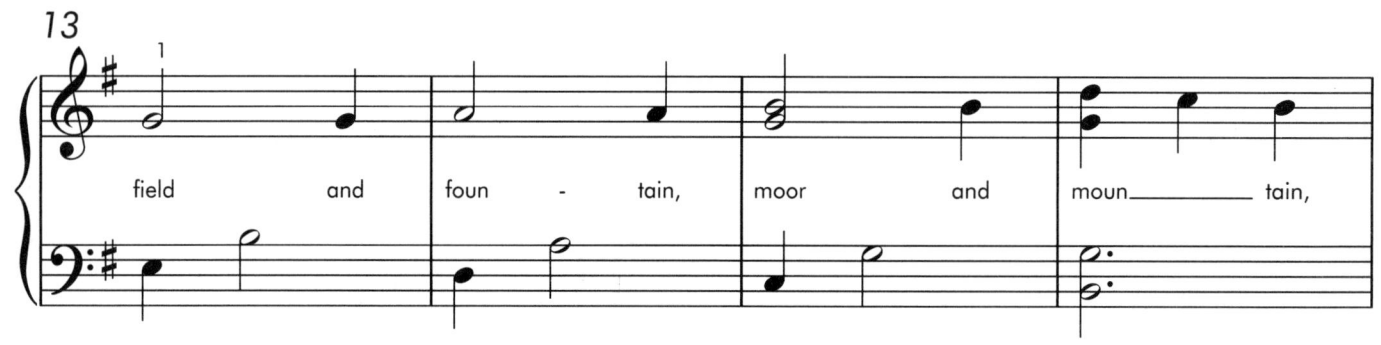

Copyright © 2018 Piano Pronto Publishing, Inc. (ASCAP)
All Rights Reserved | PianoPronto.com

We Wish You a Merry Christmas
Version 1

Traditional
Arr. Jennifer Eklund

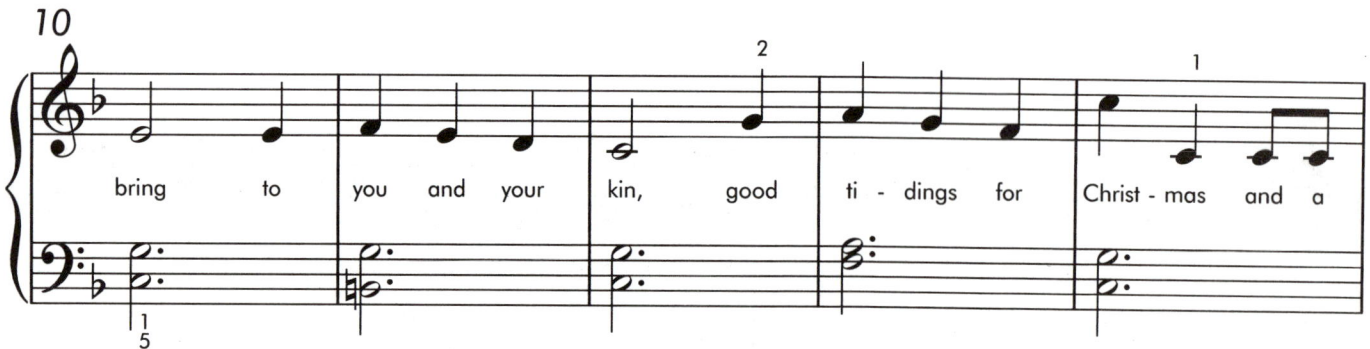

We Wish You a Merry Christmas
Version 2

Traditional
Arr. Jennifer Eklund

Joyfully

We Wish You a Merry Christmas
Version 3

Traditional
Arr. Jennifer Eklund

Joyfully

Ukrainian Bell Carol
Version 1

Mykola Leontovich
Arr. Jennifer Eklund

Quickly, in 1

with pedal

Copyright © 2018 Piano Pronto Publishing, Inc. (ASCAP)
All Rights Reserved | PianoPronto.com

Ukrainian Bell Carol
Version 2

Mykola Leontovich
Arr. Jennifer Eklund

Quickly, in 1

with pedal

Ukrainian Bell Carol
Version 3

Mykola Leontovich
Arr. Jennifer Eklund

Quickly, in 1

with pedal

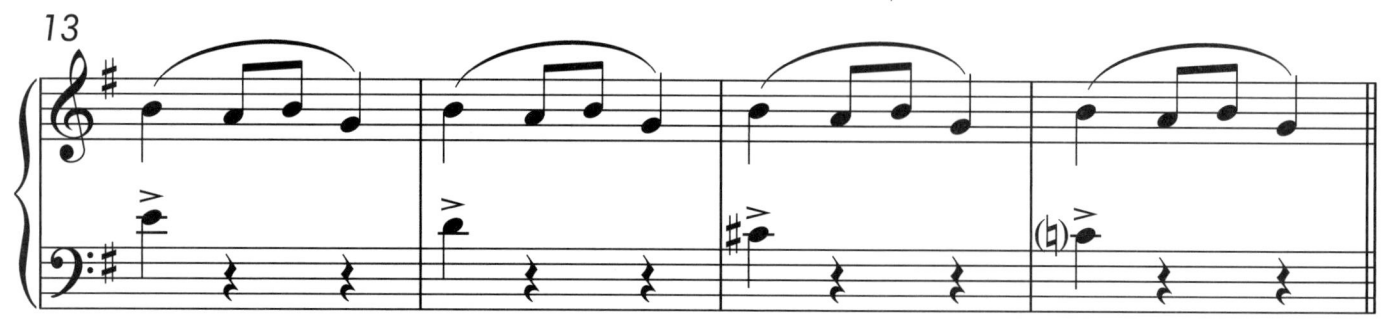

The First Noel
Version 1

Traditional
Arr. Jennifer Eklund

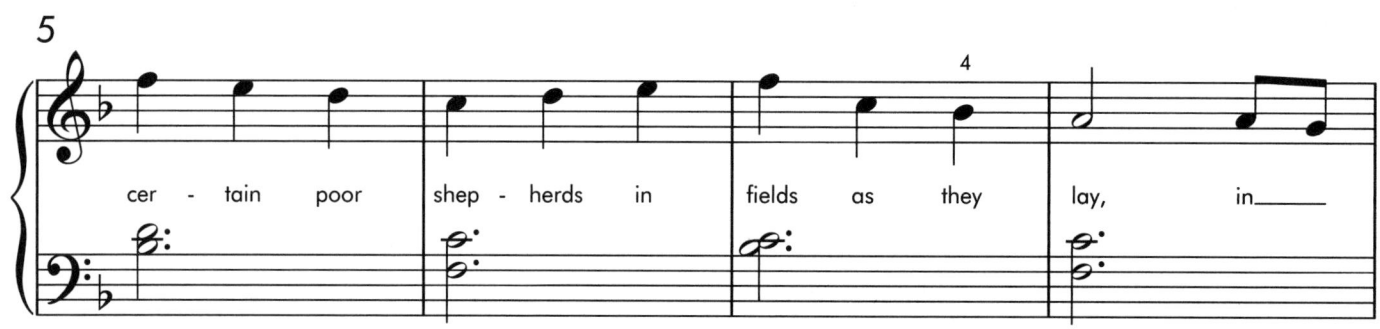
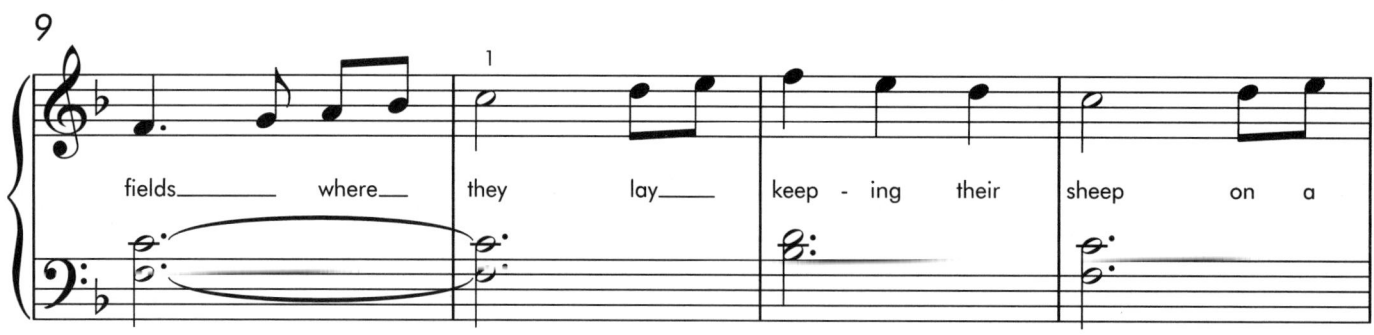

The First Noel
Version 2

Traditional
Arr. Jennifer Eklund

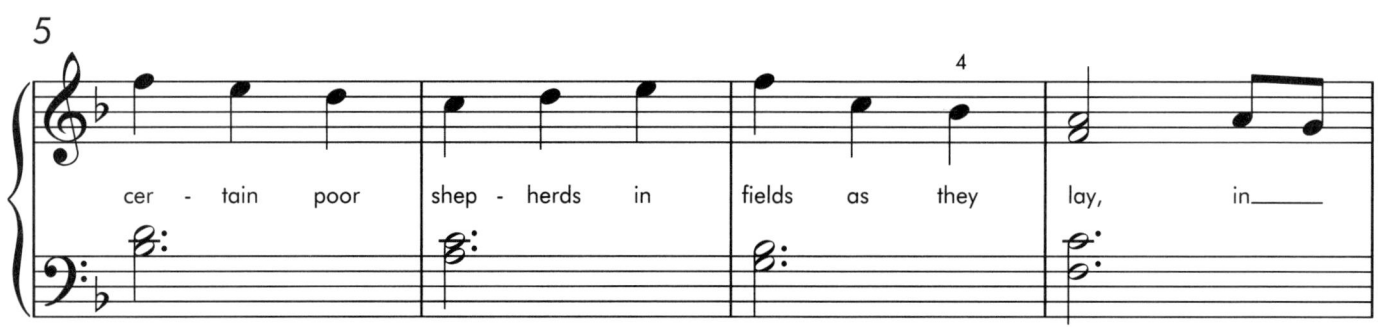
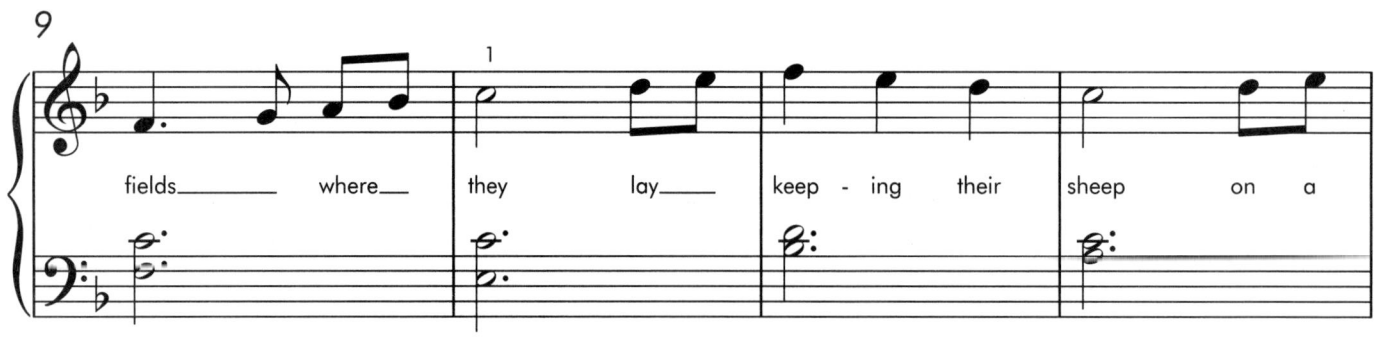

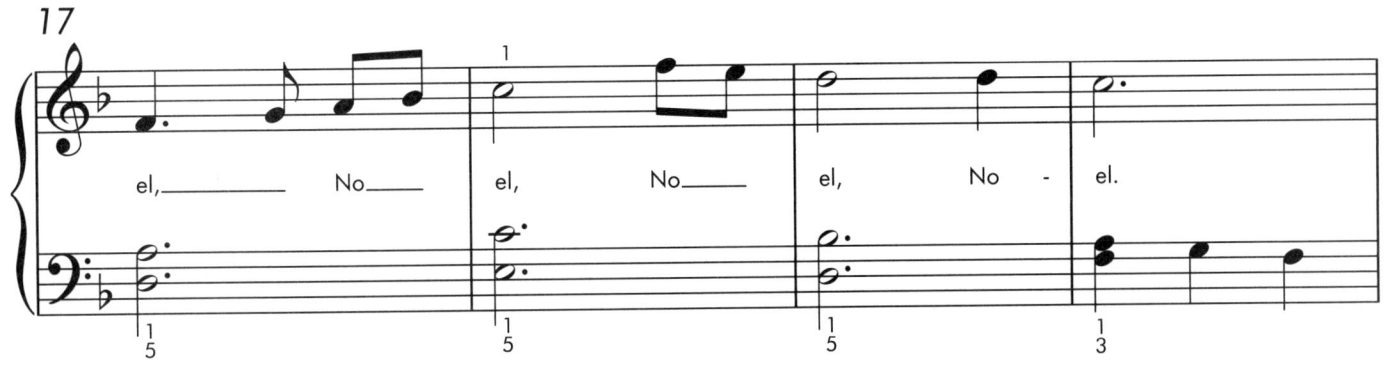
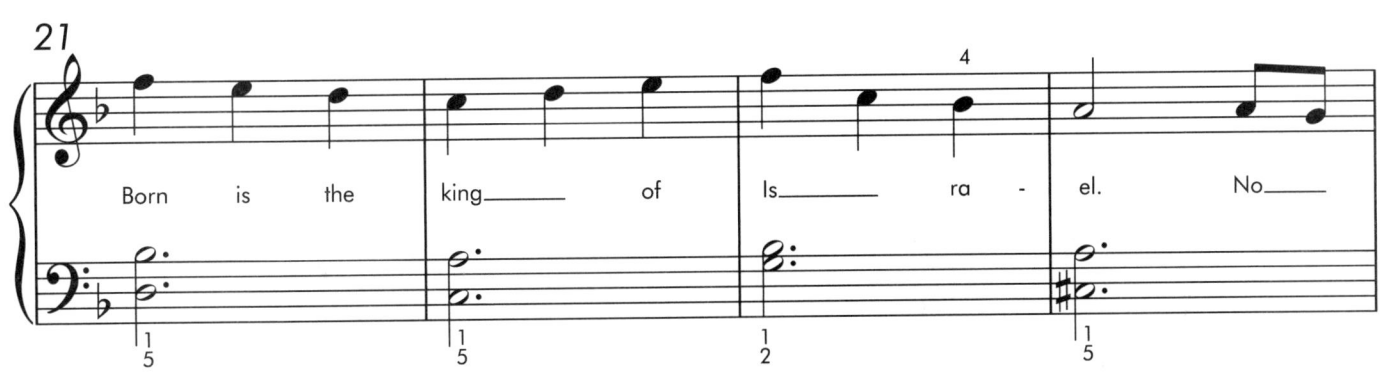

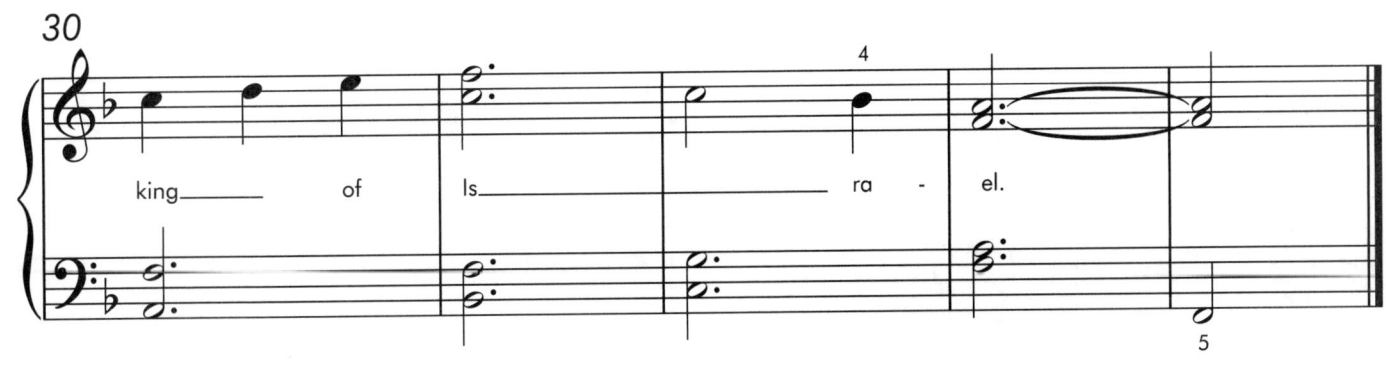

The First Noel
Version 3

Traditional
Arr. Jennifer Eklund

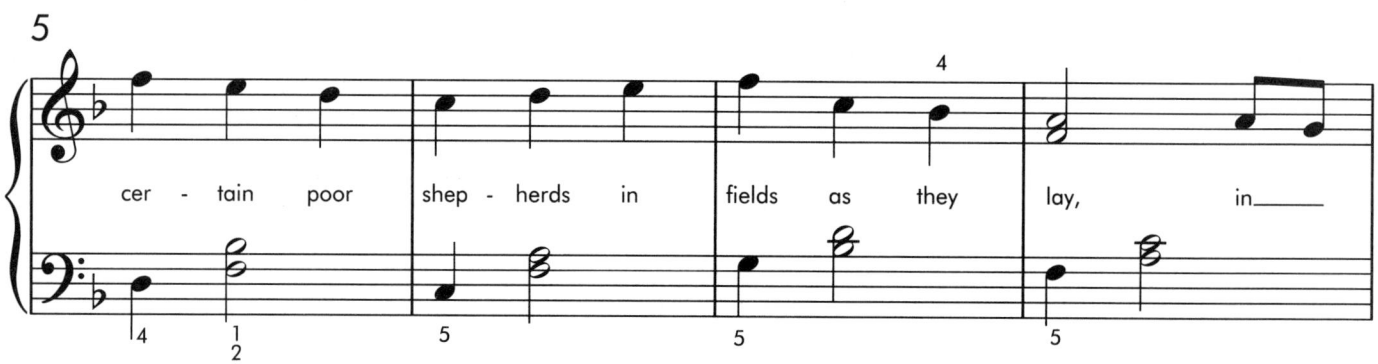
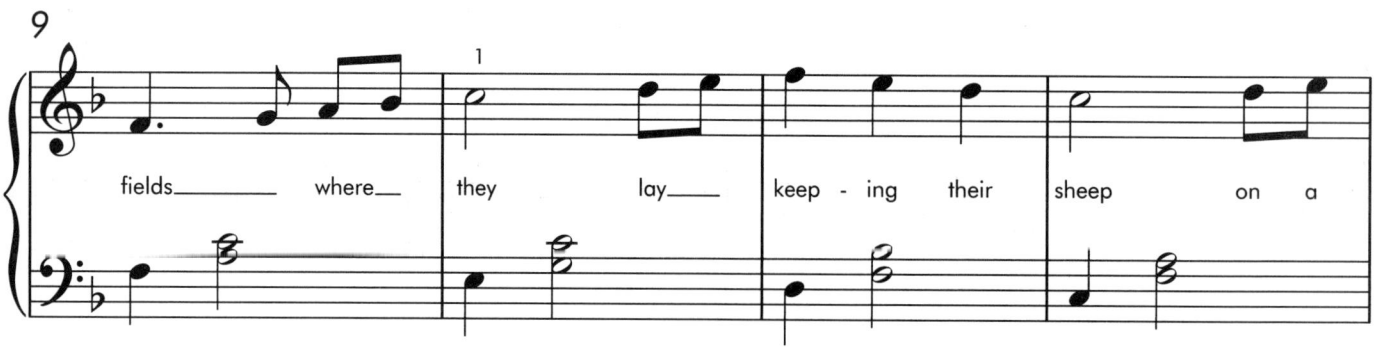
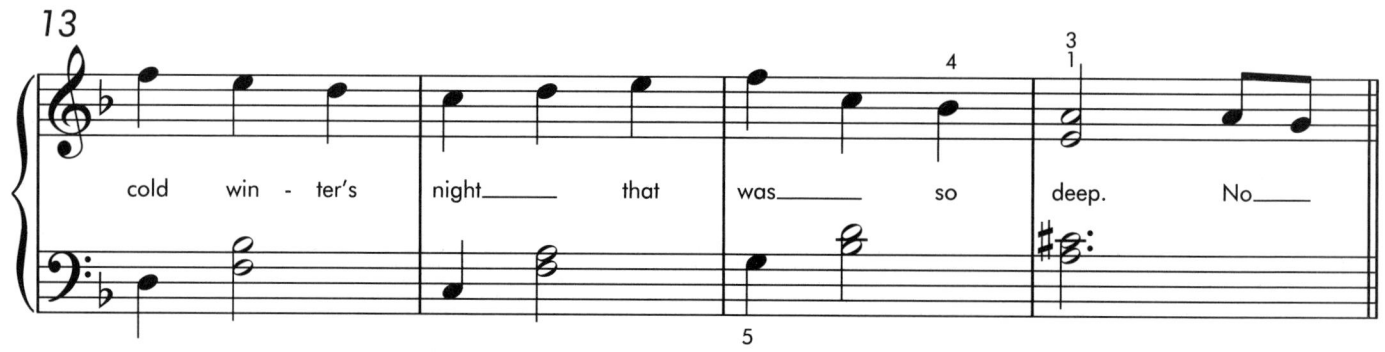

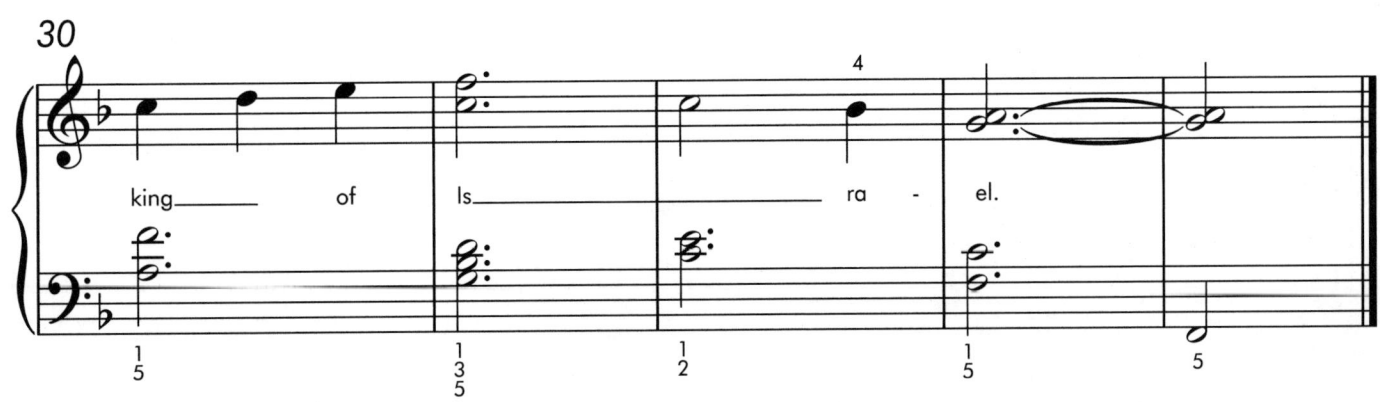

Joy to the World
Version 1

George Frideric Handel
Arr. Jennifer Eklund

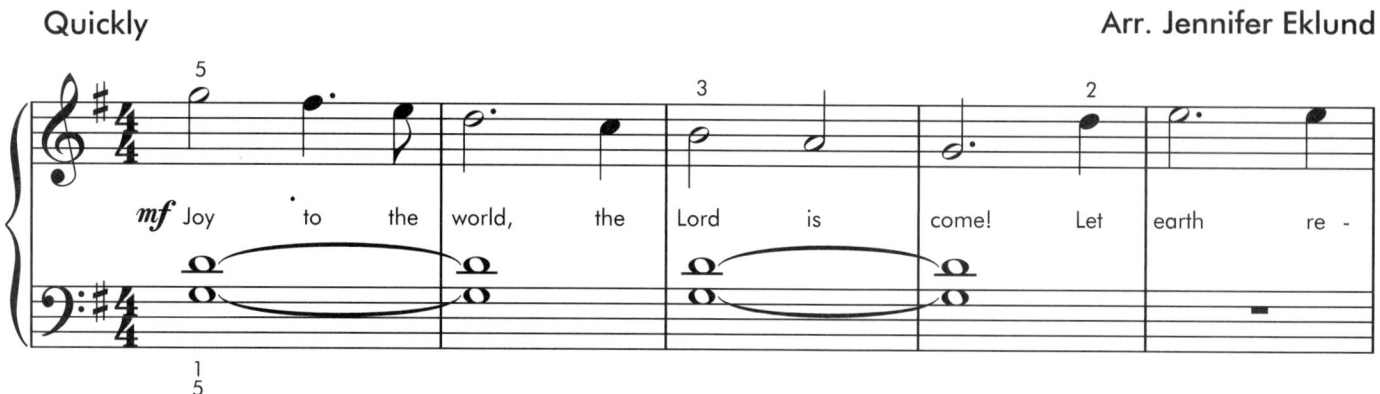
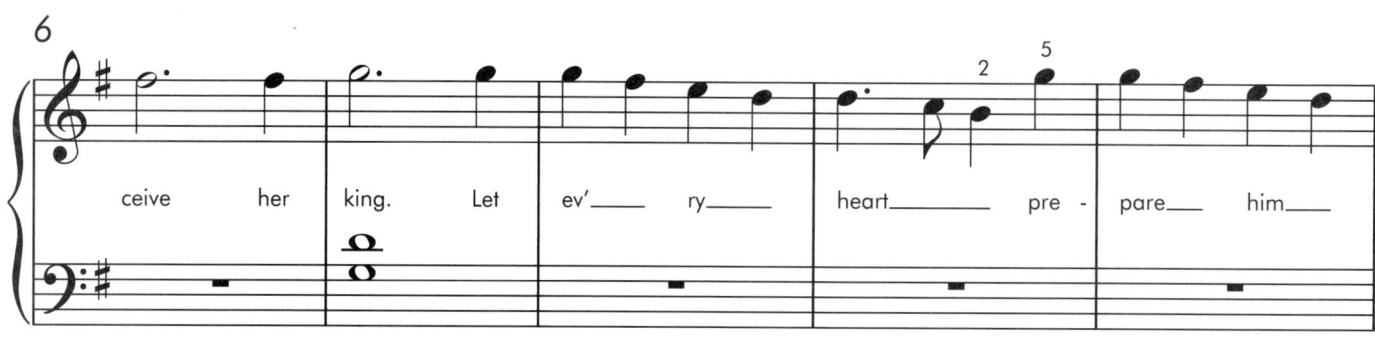

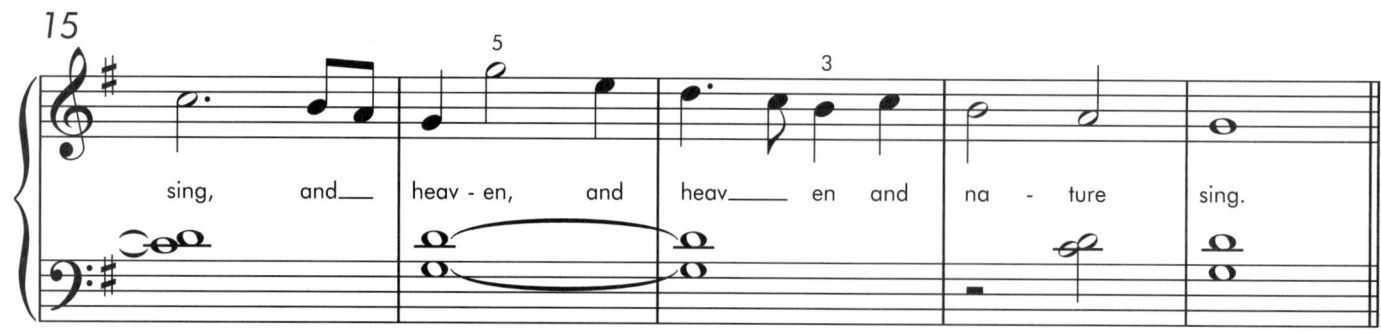

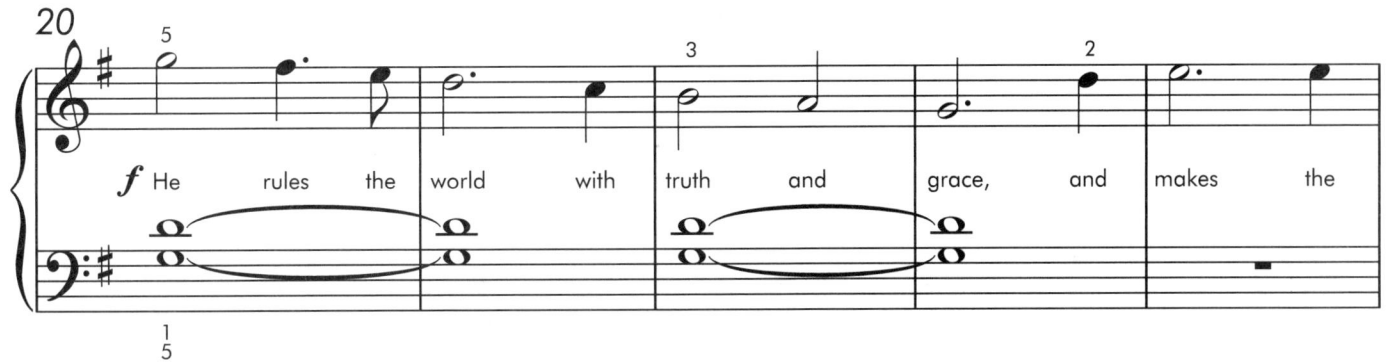
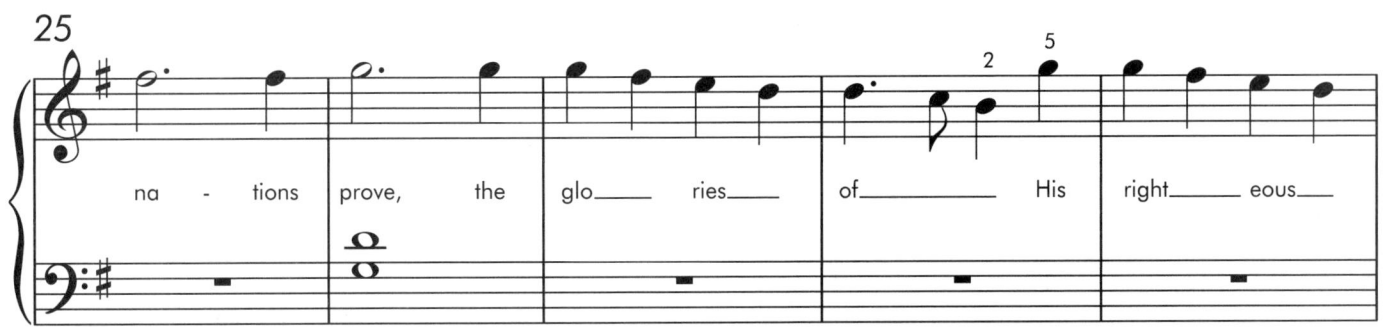
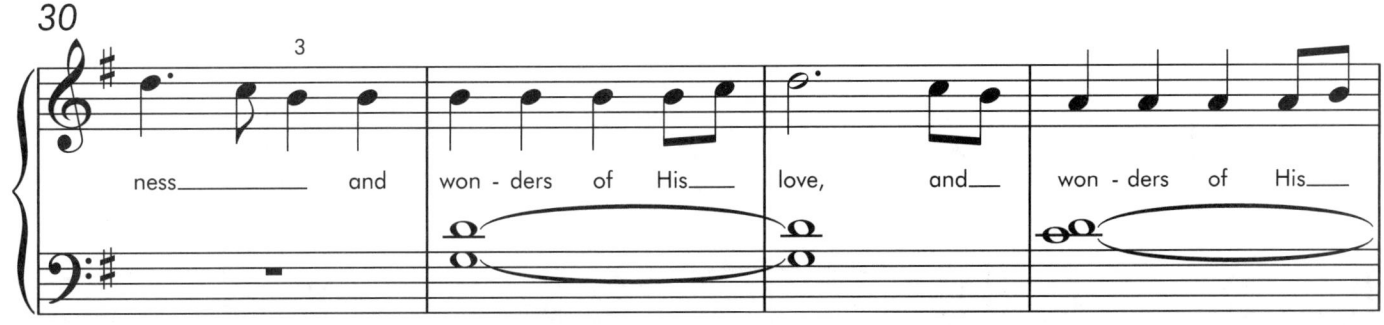
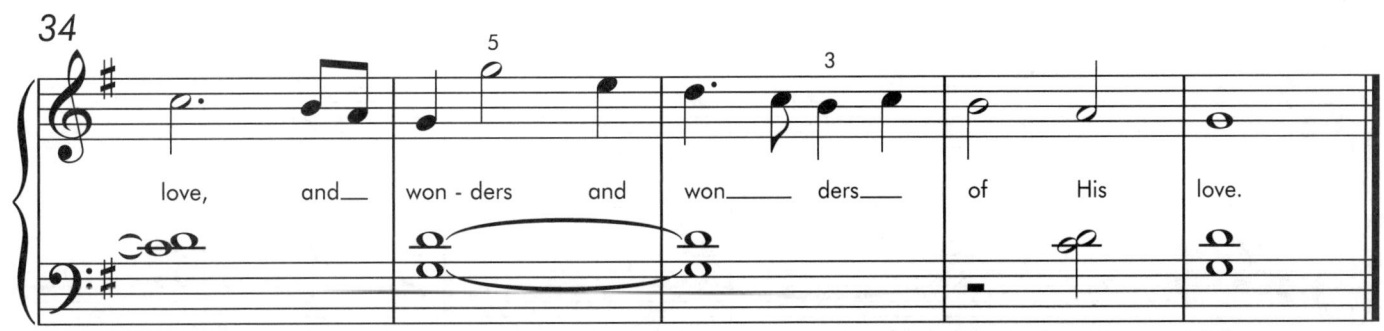

Joy to the World
Version 2

George Frideric Handel
Arr. Jennifer Eklund

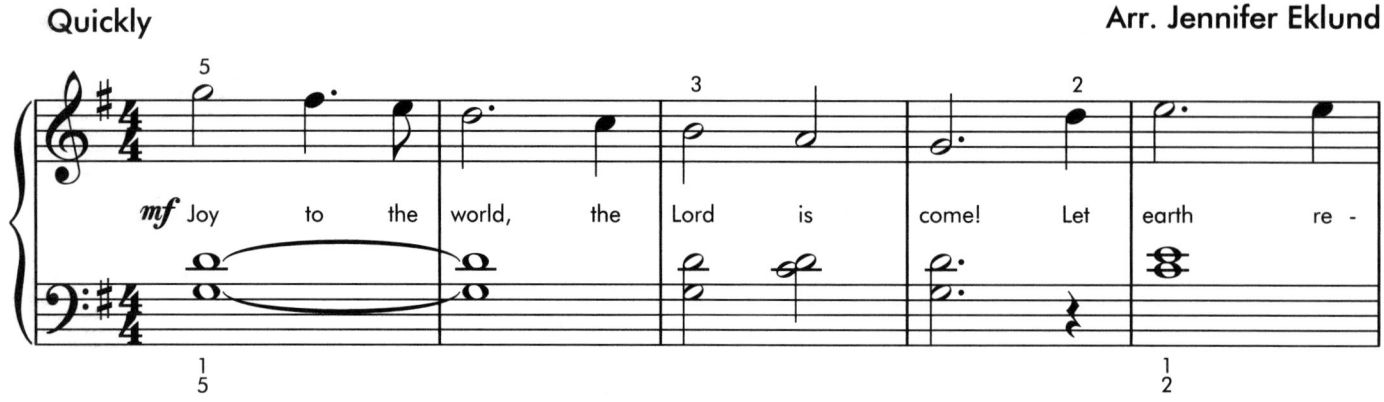
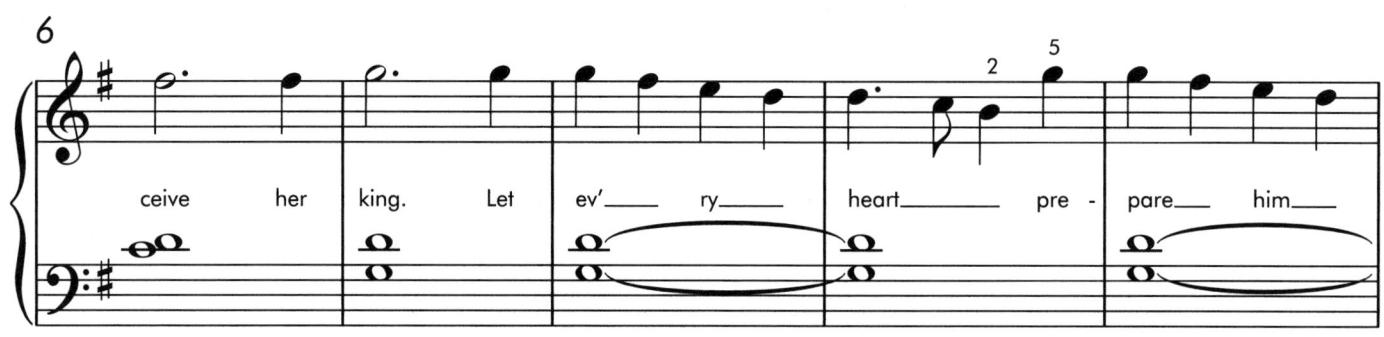

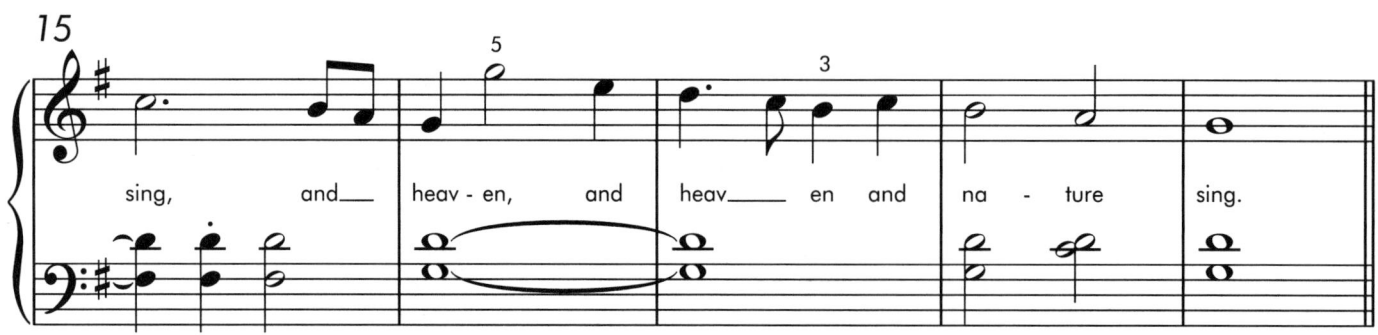

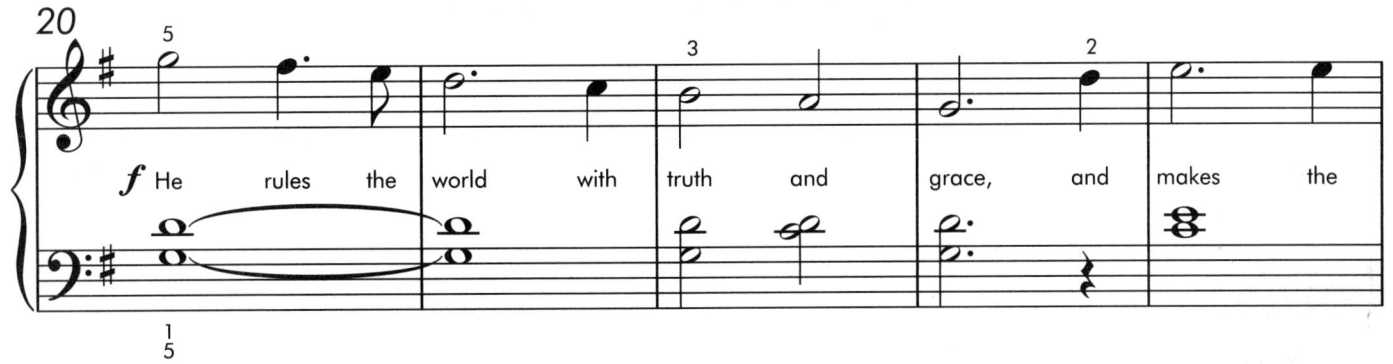

Joy to the World
Version 3

George Frideric Handel
Arr. Jennifer Eklund

Quickly

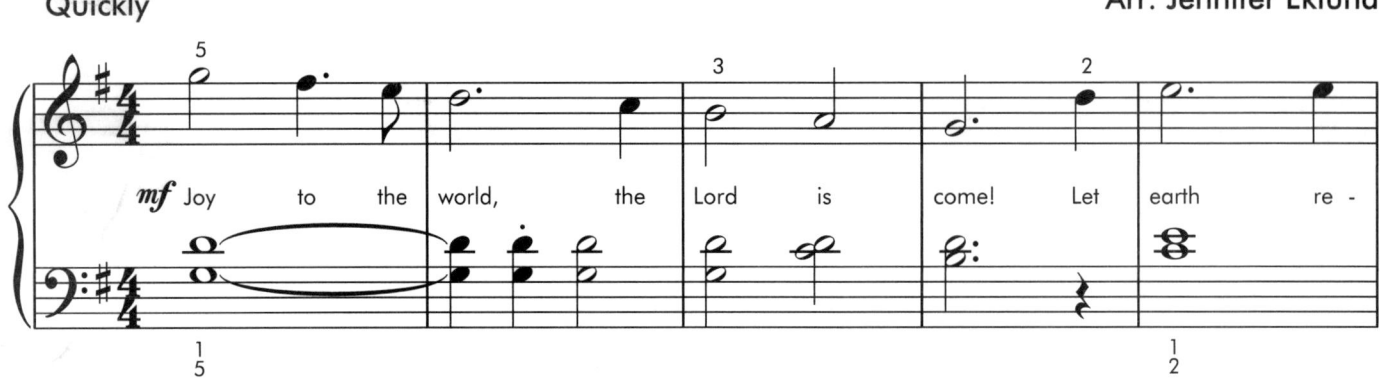
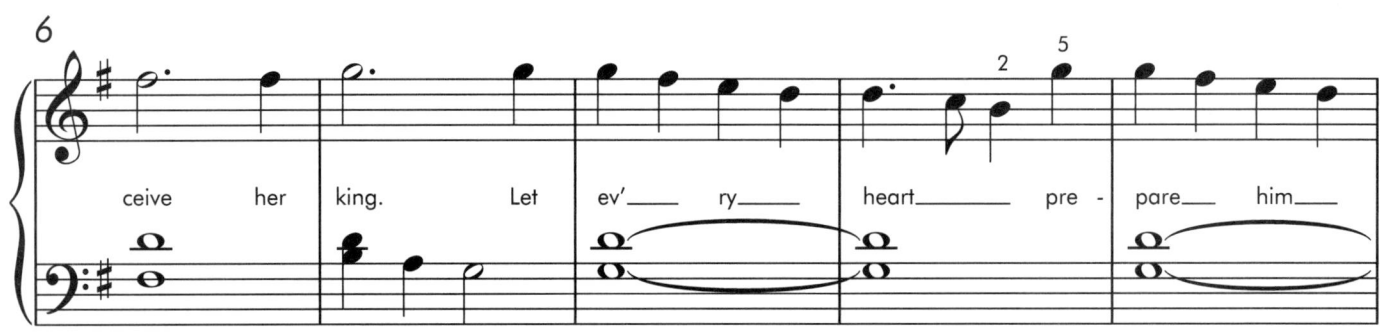
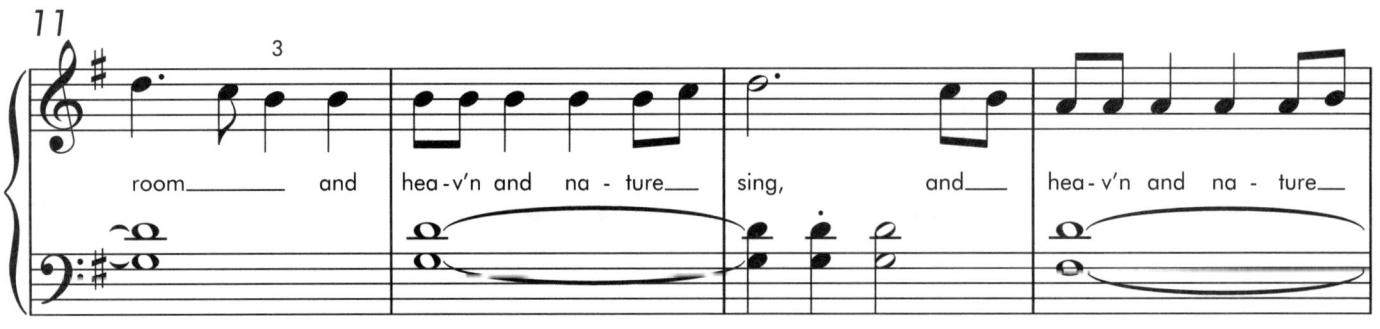
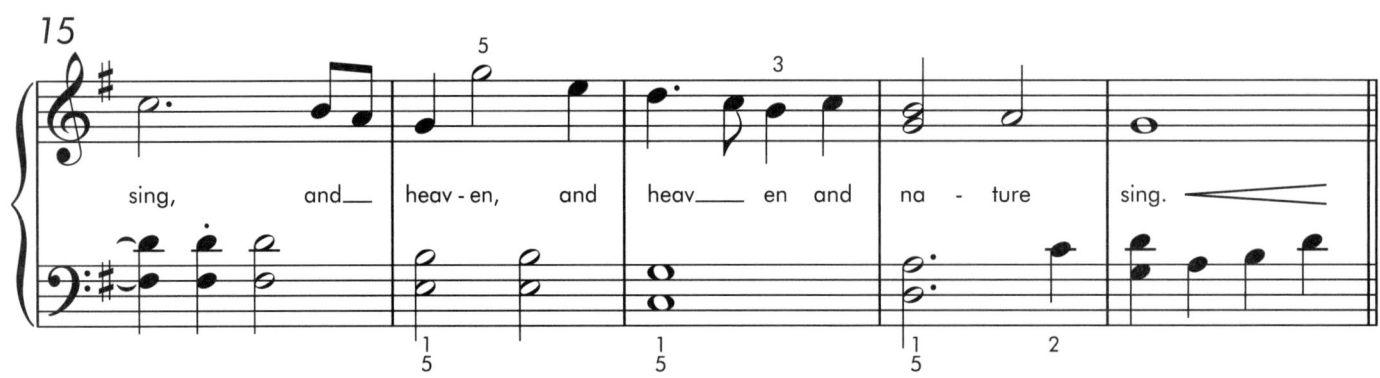

Copyright © 2018 Piano Pronto Publishing, Inc. (ASCAP)
All Rights Reserved | PianoPronto.com

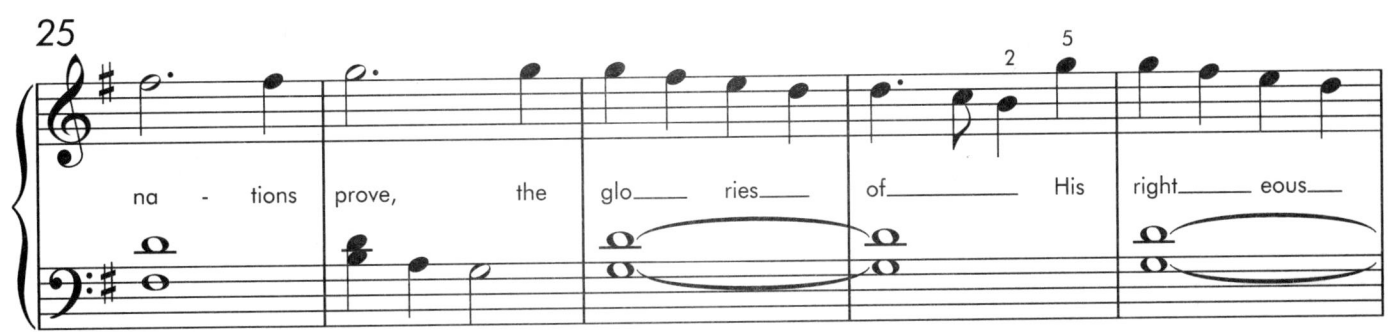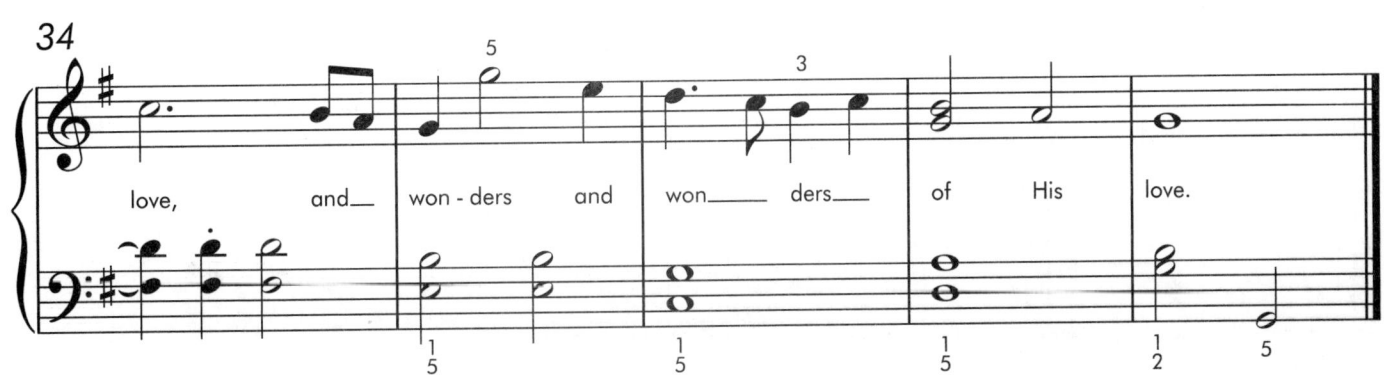

O Holy Night
Version 3

Adolphe Adam
Arr. Jennifer Eklund

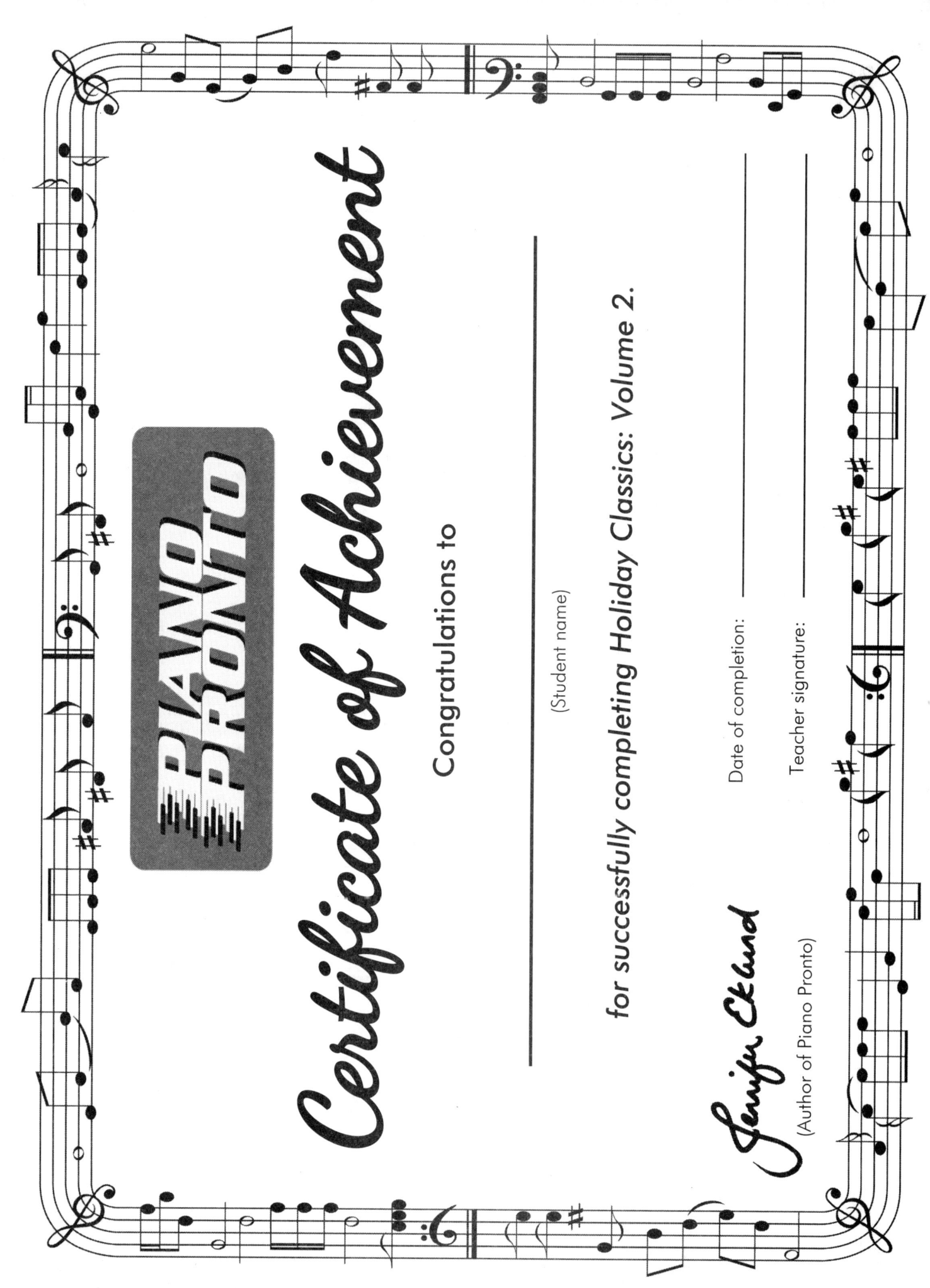